C

JUN 2015

WITHDRAWN

D1444970

Weather

BY KATHY THORNBOROUGH • ILLUSTRATIONS BY KATHLEEN PETELINSEK

The Child's World

PUBLISHED by The Child's World®
1980 Lookout Drive • Mankato, MN 56003-1705
800-599-READ • www.childsworld.com

ACKNOWLEDGMENTS
The Child's World®: Mary Berendes, Publishing Director
The Design Lab: Design
Jody Jensen Shaffer: Editing

PHOTO CREDITS
© biletskiy/Shutterstock.com: 22; Bruno Ismael Silva Alves/
Shutterstock.com: 13; Chunni4691/Shutterstock.com:L back cover,
4; ESOlex/Shutterstock.com: 11; Jan Zoetekouw/Dreamstime.com:
18; KPG Idream/Shutterstock.com: 10; maxriesgo/Shutterstock.
com: 17; Minerva Studio/Shutterstock.com: 12; Nneirda /
Shutterstock.com: 5; Nomadsoul1/iStock.com: back cover;
Oleg Hartsenko/Dreamstime.com: 1; Oleksandr Shevchenko/
Shutterstock.com: 21; Patrick Foto/Shutterstock.com: 8; ra2studio/
Shutterstock.com: 3; Rebbeck Images/Shutterstock.com: 16;
Rustle /Shutterstock.com: 19; S.Borisov /Shutterstock.com: 23;
SkylightpicturesDreamstime.com: 15; Todd Shoemake/Shutterstock.
com: cover, 1, 6; underworld/Shutterstock.com: 9; Vibrant Image
Studio: Shutterstock.com: 20; yang na/Shutterstock.com: 7

COPYRIGHT © 2015 by The Child's World®
All rights reserved. No part of this book may be reproduced or
utilized in any form or by any means without written permission
from the publisher.

ISBN 9781626873247
LCCN 2014934489

PRINTED in the United States of America
Mankato, MN
July, 2014
PA02216

A SPECIAL THANKS TO OUR ADVISERS:
As a member of a deaf family that spans four generations, Kim Bianco Majeri lives, works, and plays amongst the deaf community.

Carmine L. Vozzolo is an educator of children who are deaf and hard of hearing, as well as their families.

NOTE TO PARENTS AND EDUCATORS:
The understanding of any language begins with the acquisition of vocabulary, whether the language is spoken or manual. The books in the Talking Hands series provide readers, both young and old, with a first introduction to basic American Sign Language signs. Combining close photocues and simple, but detailed, line illustrations, children and adults alike can begin the process of learning American Sign Language. Let these books be an introduction to the world of American Sign Language. Most languages have regional dialects and multiple ways of expressing the same thought. This is also true for sign language. We have attempted to use the most common version of the signs for the words in this series. As with any language, the best way to learn is to be taught in person by a frequent user. It is our hope that this series will pique your interest in sign language.

BRAZORIA COUNTY LIBRARY
ANGLETON   TEXAS

Weather

Predicting what the weather will be is called the forecast.

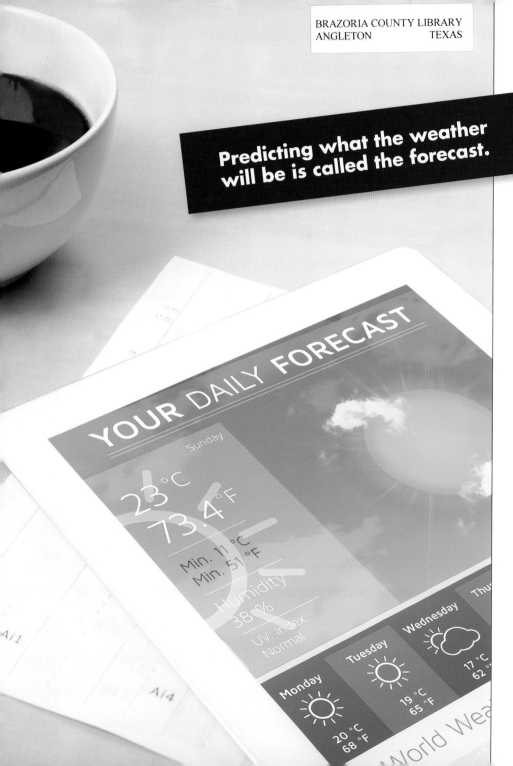

Make the "W" sign.
Then make a zigzag motion
and move your hand downward.

Temperature

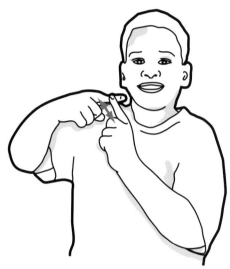

Make the "L" shape with both hands.
Your left hand points up.
Your right hand points left
and slides up and down.

4

Temperature
is measured
in Fahrenheit
and Celsius.

Flood

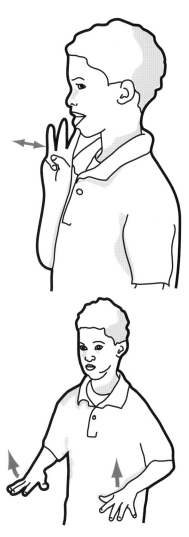

Floods cause damage all over the world.

Make the "W" shape and tap your finger to your chin. Then move your hands up as if water is rising.

Lightning

Move your right index finger
in a zigzag motion
as it moves downward.

Lightning is made
of electricity.

Thunder is caused by lightning heating the air.

Thunder

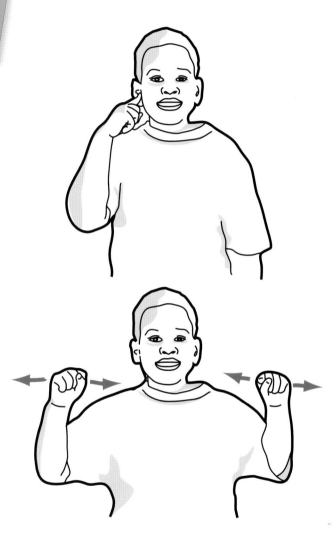

Tap your right ear with your index finger. Then move both fists right and left a few times.

Rain

Slightly curve your hands and
move them downward. Repeat.

Don't wiggle
your fingers
for this sign—
that would
mean "snow."

The highest wind speed ever recorded was 253 miles per hour (407 kmph).

Wind

Open both hands (with palms facing each other) and move them from left to right. Repeat.

Snow

Wiggle all your fingers while
moving your hands downward.

No two snowflakes
are the same.

See page 24 to learn how to make all the letters.

Ice

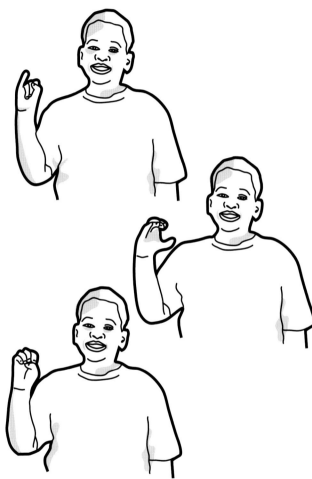

Spell I-C-E with your fingers.

11

Tornado

Open both hands and bend
your middle fingers inward.
Move your arms so your two fingers
revolve around each other—
like a tornado.

Tornadoes usually happen
between the hours of 3–9 PM.

Hurricanes are given a name to help scientists tell them apart.

Hurricane

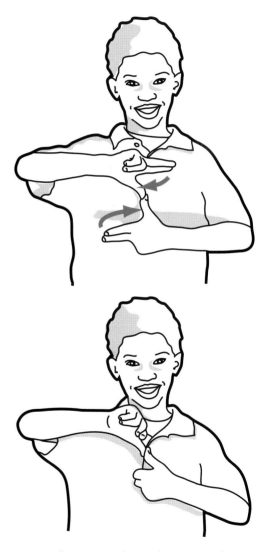

Touch your thumbs together.
Bend both index and middle fingers
over and over.

13

Sky

Spell S-K-Y with your fingers.

See page 24 to learn how to make all the letters.

Cloud

Curl your fingers and face your palms toward each other. Move both hands in a spiral motion from left to right.

Clouds are made of tiny water droplets.

15

Hot

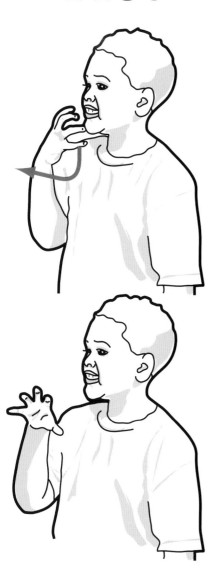

Curl your fingers toward your mouth. Move your hand down and away from your face.

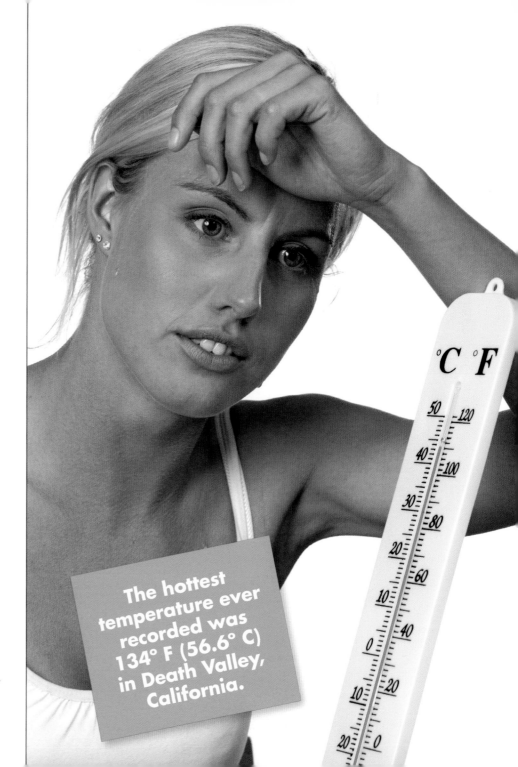

The hottest temperature ever recorded was 134° F (56.6° C) in Death Valley, California.

Cold

With both fists up,
pretend to shiver.

The coldest temperature ever recorded was -135.8° F (-93.2° C) in Antarctica.

Fog

Spell F-O-G with your fingers.

See page 24 to learn how to make all the letters.

Sunny

Sunshine helps things grow and can make people feel happy.

Touch your right thumb to your fingertips. Open your hand a little.

19

Summer

Move your right index finger from left to right across your forehead. Curl your finger when it reaches the right side.

Summer is the hottest season.

Winter is the coldest season.

Winter

Make the "W" sign and shiver
as if you are cold.

21

Spring

Put one hand around the other.
Push up like a flower blooming.

Many people think spring is their favorite season.

Leaves change color in the fall.

Fall

Hold your flat left arm like a tree.
Wave your flat right arm like
leaves falling from the tree.

23

A SPECIAL THANK YOU!

A special thank you to our models from the Program for Children Who are Deaf and Hard of Hearing at the Alexander Graham Bell Elementary School in Chicago, Illinois.

Alina's favorite things to do are art, soccer, and swimming. DJ is her brother!

Dareous likes football. His favorite team is the Detroit Lions. He also likes to play video games.

DJ loves playing the harmonica and video games. Alina is his sister!